*Dedicated in Loving Memory of my
Mother and Grandmother,
Emily Ann Baldwin Fuller and
Vesta Crayton Fuller
and
to the best Daddy in the world,
Henry B. Fuller.*

My Mama Taught Me Better Than That!

Heidi B. Fuller

My Mama Taught Me Better Than That!
Copyright © 2015 by Heidi B. Fuller

Book Illustrations by: Ms. V
Book Servicing by: B.O.S.S. Publishing
Edited by: Aunt Winnie

All rights reserved.

No part of this book may be reproduced, scanned, or distributed in any form or manner whatsoever without written permission from Publishing agents, or author.

All quotes mentioned in this book are for entertainment purposes only and are not meant to give credit or take credit away from anyone.

For information, contact: heidibfuller@hotmail.com

For information regarding special discounts for bulk purchases, sales, promotions, speaking engagements and or book clubs, please contact us by email at: heidibfuller@hotmail.com

Manufactured in the United States of America

ISBN: 978-0986355974

10 9 8 7 6 5 4 3 2

INTRODUCTION

As an eager dad raced through the busy airport, excited to see his darling daughter, he realized he had no gift for which to welcome her home. He glanced into the glass window of a tiny shop. Looking back at him was the perfect book fit for a princess to inspire, encourage, uplift and make her smile entitled: "My Mama Taught Me Better Than That" and this was my God-given vision…

The words that we speak are powerful. They can build us up or tear us down—be sweet like honey or bitter like tea—make us feel like a failure or become fuel for feeling victorious. This light-hearted book is full of phrases that will enlighten, empower and make you laugh out loud. They are reassuring and thought-provoking expressions that have rolled off our tongues for decades! This book was a true eye opener for me and is sure to be for many others. As parents, mentors and leaders, we must make a conscious effort to say things that will allow our children, and those who cross our path, to grow and be functional citizens in today's society. No matter what color, creed or nationality, we all want the same things for ourselves and our families—to be happy and loved.

I thank God for the vision and opportunity to dedicate my first book to my loved ones: Henry B. and Ester Fuller, Yvette M. McMillan, Ramraghi V. Fuller, Donovan J. Hunter and Chase A. Ponder. Last, but certainly not least, to my precious and beautiful children, Hunter Fuller Reed and Madison Bene't White. —Truly, all I do is for you.

~Fairy Dust~

It's that "mommy smell" I remember most—your sweet aroma in the air…
For all the times you had my back; showed just how much you care.
You believed in me against all odds; taught me to spread my wings and fly…
For truly yours were the Angel's wings I mounted to soar on high.
I miss the days of hanging out—your loving laughter—you and me…
The cherished bond built with my children; now I behold, I see.
Because of you, I embrace the thought that I can do anything!
Because of your steadfast prayers for me, I have a song to sing.
Like Emily Ann's fairy dust, you softly covered my life with joy…
And I thank the Good Lord for our 'girly chats' I used to so enjoy.
I learned from you to be kind, be me, a fabulously-fierce-kind-of-girl…
To sprinkle my anointed dust upon others; to encourage a better world.
Yes, you and Grandmamma—awesomely stylish—true Princesses; beautiful; bold…
A powerful legacy; a fruitful life; a story yet untold.
For all the days you worried, Mama, please forgive me, I didn't know…
How much you deeply loved me—and now how much greater I Love You so.

By Carolyn A. Watson © 2015

629
phrases you can expect to hear from your mother, sister, auntie, girlfriend or someone who cares about you in your lifetime...

"Be a problem solver."

"Be anxious for nothing."
(Phil 4:6)

"Be all that YOU can be."

"Be a team player."

"Be nice to everyone. It's the right thing to do."

"Be comfortable in your own skin."

"Be effective."

"Be excited!!!"

"Be open and willing."

My Mama Taught Me Better Than That!

"Be happy!!!"

"Be grateful."

"Be thankful."

"Be a good friend."

"Be still!"

"Be forgiving."

"Be a leader."

"Be prepared."

"Be nice to your sister/brother."

"Be early."
(be on time)."

"Be so happy that when others look at you, they become happy too"

"Be the star that you are."

My Mama Taught Me Better Than That!

"Be independent."

"Be patient."

"There will never be another you."

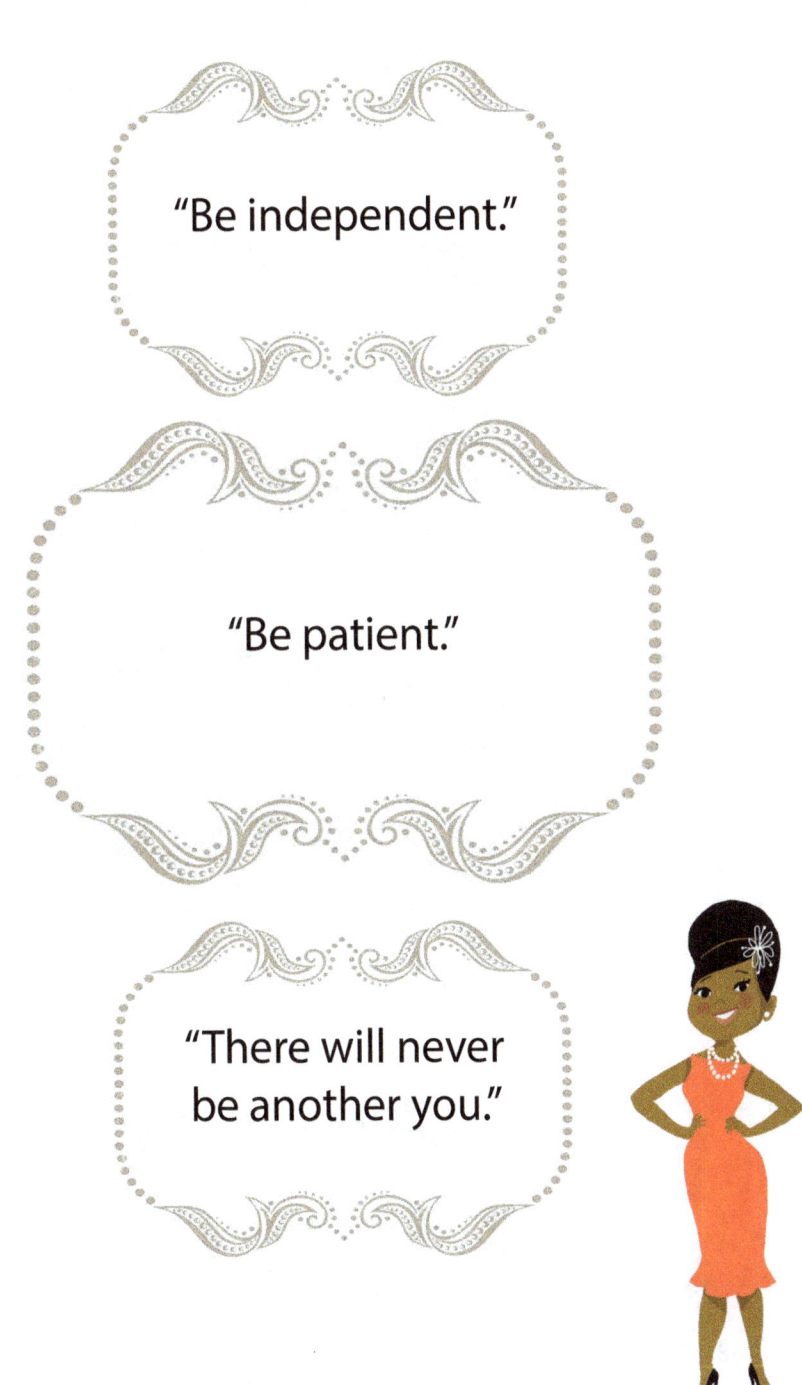

"Be optimistic."

"Be a trusted friend."

"Be kind."

"Be happy for others."

"Be the best at whatever you do."

"Be encouraged"

"Be grateful."

"Be happy with yourself, by yourself."

"Be consistent."

My Mama Taught Me Better Than That!

"Be good to people."

"Be true to what God put in your heart."

"Believe in you."

"Be amazing."

"Be the kind of person people want to be around."

My Mama said...

"As a man thinks in his heart so is he."
(Prov 23:7)

"Act like you are already there."

"All money ain't good money."

"Let people miss you."
(You don't want it to be said, 'He's at every party').

"People will tell you you can't but baby, you can."

My Mama Taught Me Better Than That!

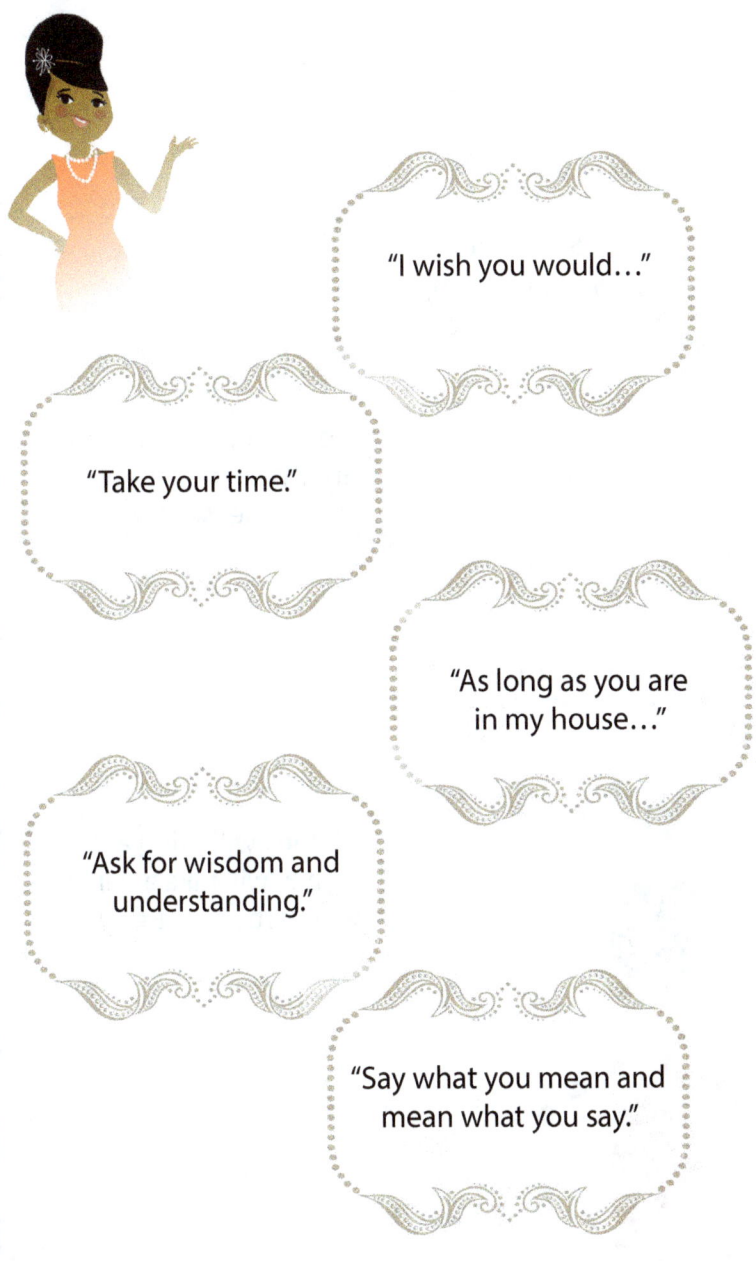

"I wish you would…"

"Take your time."

"As long as you are in my house…"

"Ask for wisdom and understanding."

"Say what you mean and mean what you say."

"Someone is always watching."

"Some people will come into your life only for a season."

"Know when to let go."

"If they will bring a tail, they will take a tail."
- Barbera W. Berry

"Live life to the fullest."

"Relationships change, people grow."

"Everybody who looks grown is not necessarily an adult."

"Fall in LOVE."

"Whatever it is, with God on our side, we can handle it."

"Pay attention to the details."

"Find a need, fill a need."
(Robots the movie)

"Go get my belt!!!"

"Try not to build walls."

"What you expect, you will get."

"Some people are just angry and mad. Don't take it personally. (They are afraid)."

My Mama Taught Me Better Than That!

"Work to learn."

"I'm only going to say this once."

"Mind yo' own business."

"Take Action."

"God has not given us a spirit of fear, but of power and love and a sound mind." - (2Tim 1:7)

"The best is yet to come."

"CYA"
(Cover your ass)

"Keep your eye on the prize."

"Please speak correct English."

"Expect great things in your life."

My Mama Taught Me Better Than That!

"It's POSSIBLE."

"Make each day count."

"Keep your eyes wide open."

"It's all about people."

"Put some money away."

My Mama Taught Me Better Than That!

"Tell the truth."

"Answer your phone' I pay that bill too.'"

"Not another word."

"I will slap the taste outcha mouth."

"There's always more."

My Mama Taught Me Better Than That!

"How many times have I told you…?"

"I should never have to come home to a dirty house."

"Watch your mouth."

"Laugh out loud."

"Clean your room."

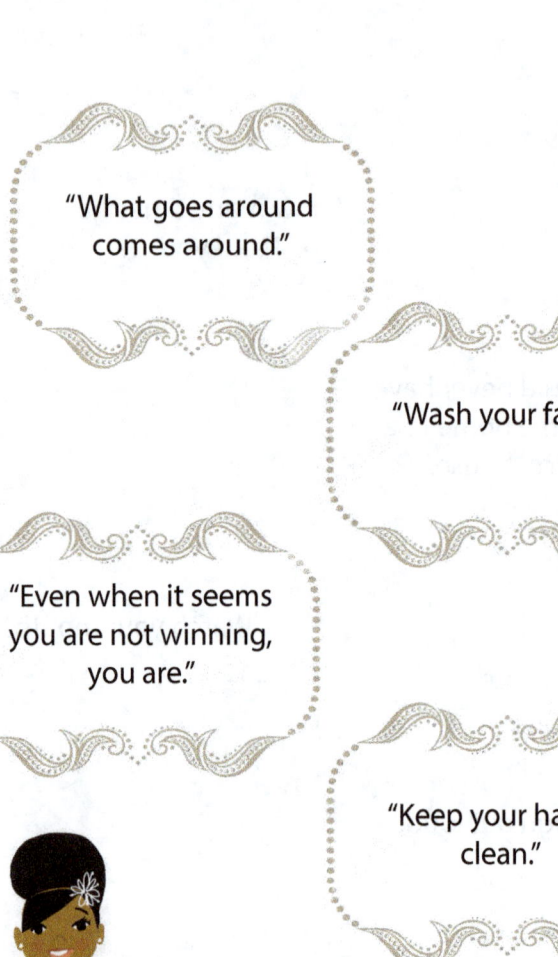

"What goes around comes around."

"Wash your face."

"Even when it seems you are not winning, you are."

"Keep your hands clean."

"No good thing shall be withheld from you as long as you walk with integrity."- (Psalms 84:11)

My Mama Taught Me Better Than That!

"Quitters never win and winners never quit!!!"

"Nothing lacking. Nothing missing (you have everything you need inside of you to win)."

"Look people in the eye."

"God is on your side."

"Finish YOUR race."

My Mama Taught Me Better Than That!

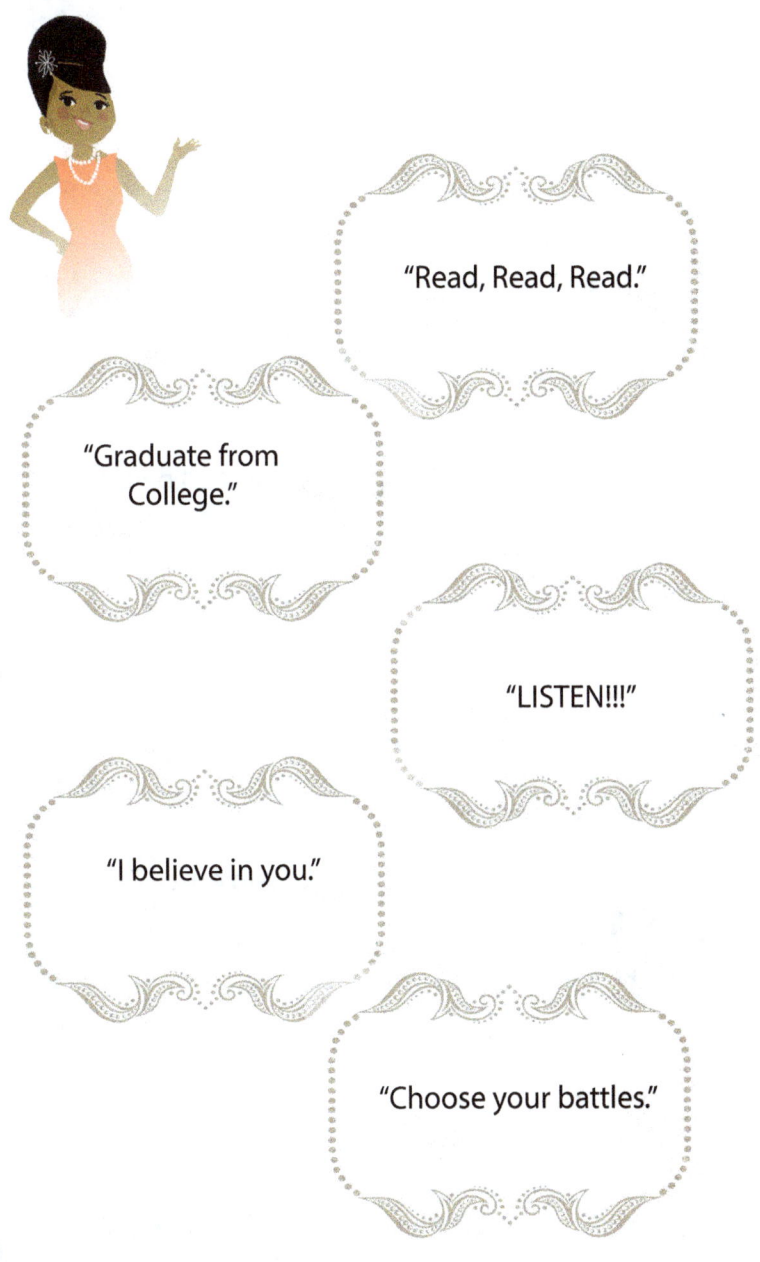

"Read, Read, Read."

"Graduate from College."

"LISTEN!!!"

"I believe in you."

"Choose your battles."

My Mama Taught Me Better Than That!

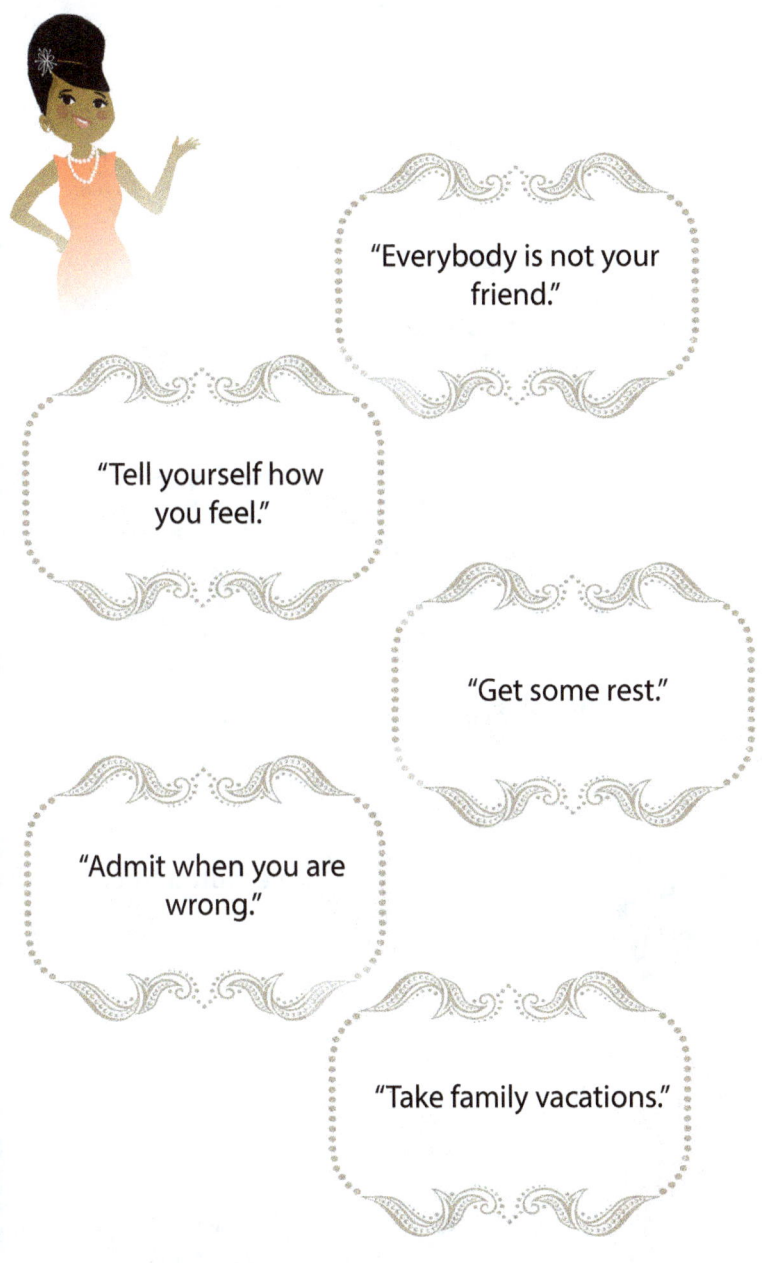

"Everybody is not your friend."

"Tell yourself how you feel."

"Get some rest."

"Admit when you are wrong."

"Take family vacations."

"Do's & Don't..."

"Do it right the first time."

"Don't speak when adults are talking."

"Don't burn bridges."

"Don't judge anyone."

"Don't pop gum."

"Don't expect a pat on the back."

"Don't waver."

"Don't take the car."

"Don't grow up so fast."

"Don't tell all yo' business."

"Don't make excuses."

"Don't make me have to come back there, call you again or get up."

"Don't believe everything you read."

"Don't worry about it."

"Don't go to bed angry with anyone."

"Do what is right."

"Don't be a garden tool. Be the prize."

"Don't give up."

"Don't talk too much."

"Don't ever have to apologize for the way you look."

"Do it afraid."

"Do I have to hear your music through your headphones?"

"Don't hold on to old stuff."

"Don't let anything take you out."

"Don't talk yourself out of a good thing."

"Don't volunteer information."

"Don't ever quit."

"Don't steal."

"Don't lie to yourself."

"Don't sit so close to the TV or computer."

"Don't text and drive."

"Don't touch a black girl's (women's) hair."

"Don't drink and drive."

"Don't drink."

"Don't do drugs, shoot heroin, pop pills, snort cocaine, or anything that will kill you"

"Don't talk too much."

"Don't let disappointments keep you down."

"Don't cheat."

"Don't lie."

"Don't be a part of someone else's pain."

"Don't hold back."

"Don't be selfish."

"Don't get distracted."

"Don't use that tone of voice with me."

"Don't let how you feel keep you from doing what is right."

"Don't talk about people."

"Don't let your mouth get you in trouble."

"Don't look at me like that."

"Don't smoke."

"Don't talk back to me."

"Don't take life for granted."

"Don't be the person no one wants to be around (negative)."

"Don't you rush to get old."

"Don't be two-faced."

"Don't lock that door!"

"Do it today!!!"

"Don't do something you will be ashamed of."

"Don't tell everything."

"Don't whisper in front of people. It's rude,"

"Don't touch nothing. Don't ask for nothing."

"Don't chase after boys."

"Do your best."

"Don't be late for everything."

"Don't get discouraged."

"Don't live to please people; live to please God."

"Don't be greedy."

"Don't settle for less when God made you for so much more."

"Do your part."

"Don't be afraid to ask."

"Don't make a meal out of those chips."

My Mama said...

(Part 2)

My Mama Taught Me Better Than That!

"Keep a smile on your face and a song in your heart."

"Have a plan ,write the plan, do the plan."

"Fear nothing but standing still."
(Tia Jakes)

"Chew with your mouth closed."

"Study to show yourself approved unto God."
- (2 Tim. 2:15, KJV)

"Take a class."

"Keep a journal."

"Finish!!!"

"Stay fit, take care of your body."

"Who's the best mommy in the whole wide world?"
- Yvette M. McMillan

My Mama Taught Me Better Than That!

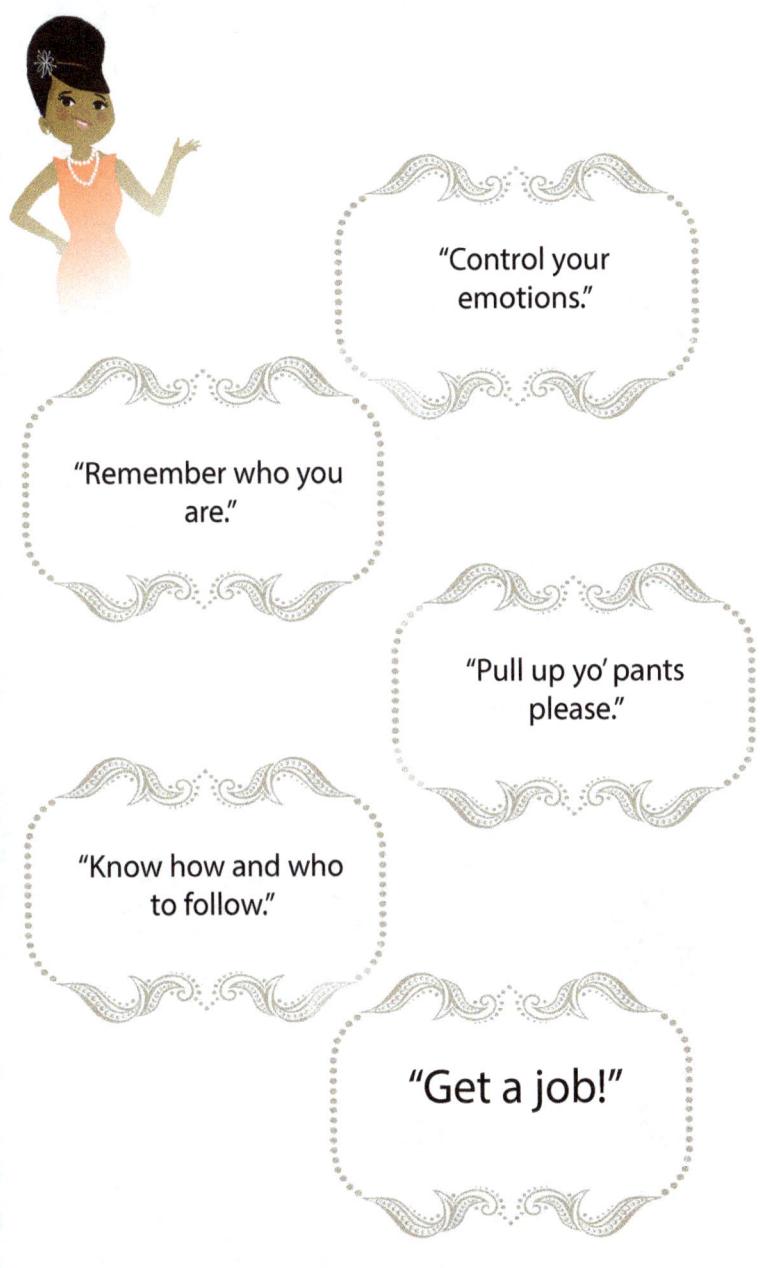

"Control your emotions."

"Remember who you are."

"Pull up yo' pants please."

"Know how and who to follow."

"Get a job!"

My Mama Taught Me Better Than That!

"Yes Sir. No Sir."

"Look at ME when I'm talking to you."

"Know when to go home."

"Say please and thank you."

My Mama Taught Me Better Than That!

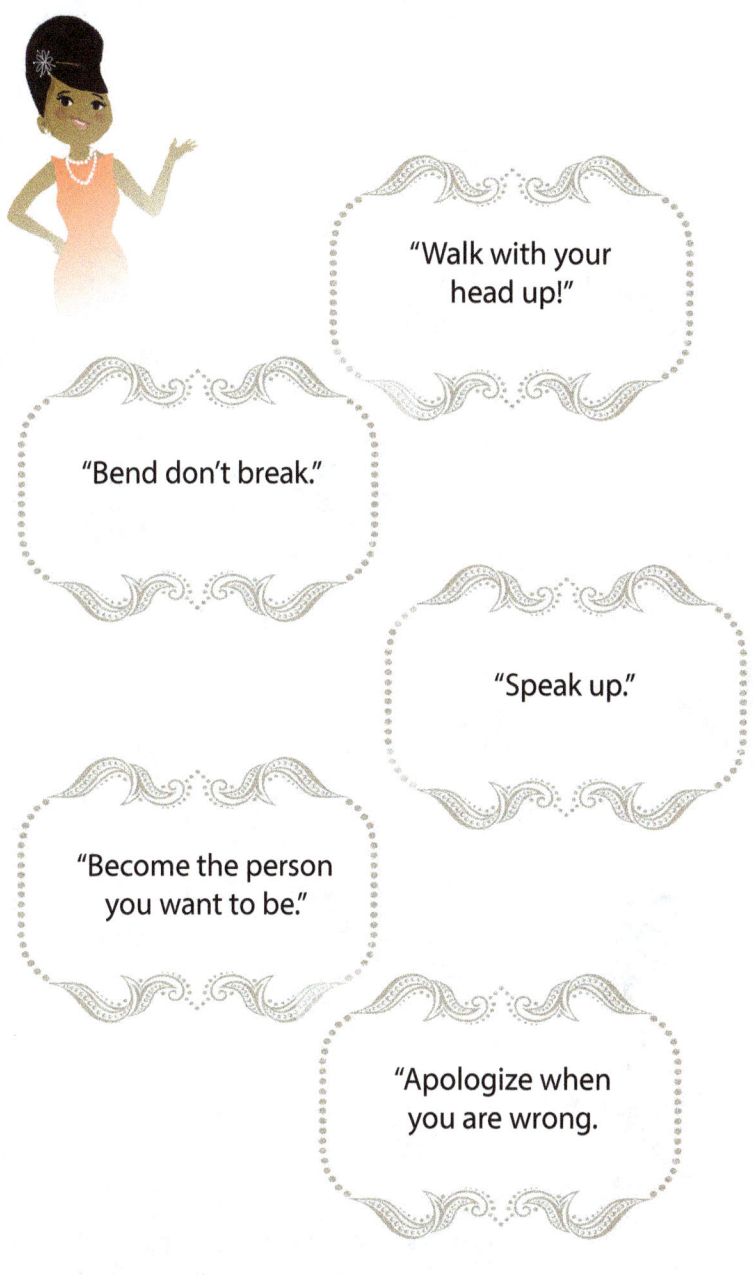

"Walk with your head up!"

"Bend don't break."

"Speak up."

"Become the person you want to be."

"Apologize when you are wrong.

My Mama Taught Me Better Than That!

"Rise up."

"God will supply your every need."

"God is with you; NOTHING can stop you."

"Call on the Lord."

"Have hope."

"Sing a new song."

"Give God ALL the glory."

"He loves you. He created you."

"ALL things are possible if you believe."
(Matt 19:26)

"Check the man in the mirror (Ask yourself is it me that's causing the problem?)."

My Mama Taught Me Better Than That!

"Stop telling people more than they need to know."

"Smell good."

"Read the Bible."

"I like you."

"Life is what you make it and it can be spectacular!!!"

"Shortcuts make long delays."

"Worship the Lord."

"Watch what comes out of your mouth."

"Make a joyful noise."

"Live to give. It will always come back in one form or another."

My Mama Taught Me Better Than That!

"Pray, Pray, Pray."

"Marry who you love."

"Seek God everyday, first thing in the morning."

"Praise Him always."

"Purchase good shoes."

My Mama Taught Me Better Than That!

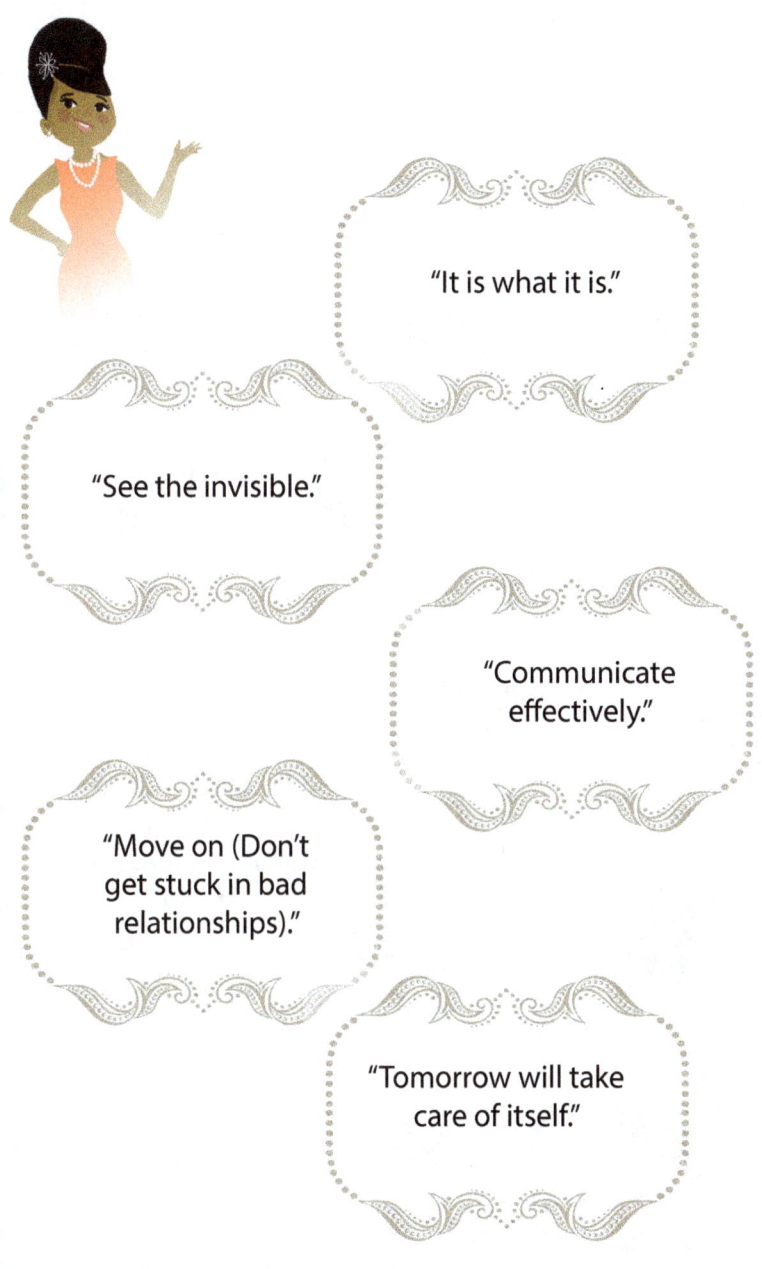

"It is what it is."

"See the invisible."

"Communicate effectively."

"Move on (Don't get stuck in bad relationships)."

"Tomorrow will take care of itself."

My Mama Taught Me Better Than That!

"Play to WIN!!!"

"Work at life everyday."

"When you wake up happy, you will be happy."

"Work at being happy."

My Mama Taught Me Better Than That!

"Let go and let God." - (Grandmama)

"Trust in the Lord."

"Forgive yourself."

"I want you."

"It's easy to stand with the crowd. It takes courage to stand alone."

My Mama Taught Me Better Than That!

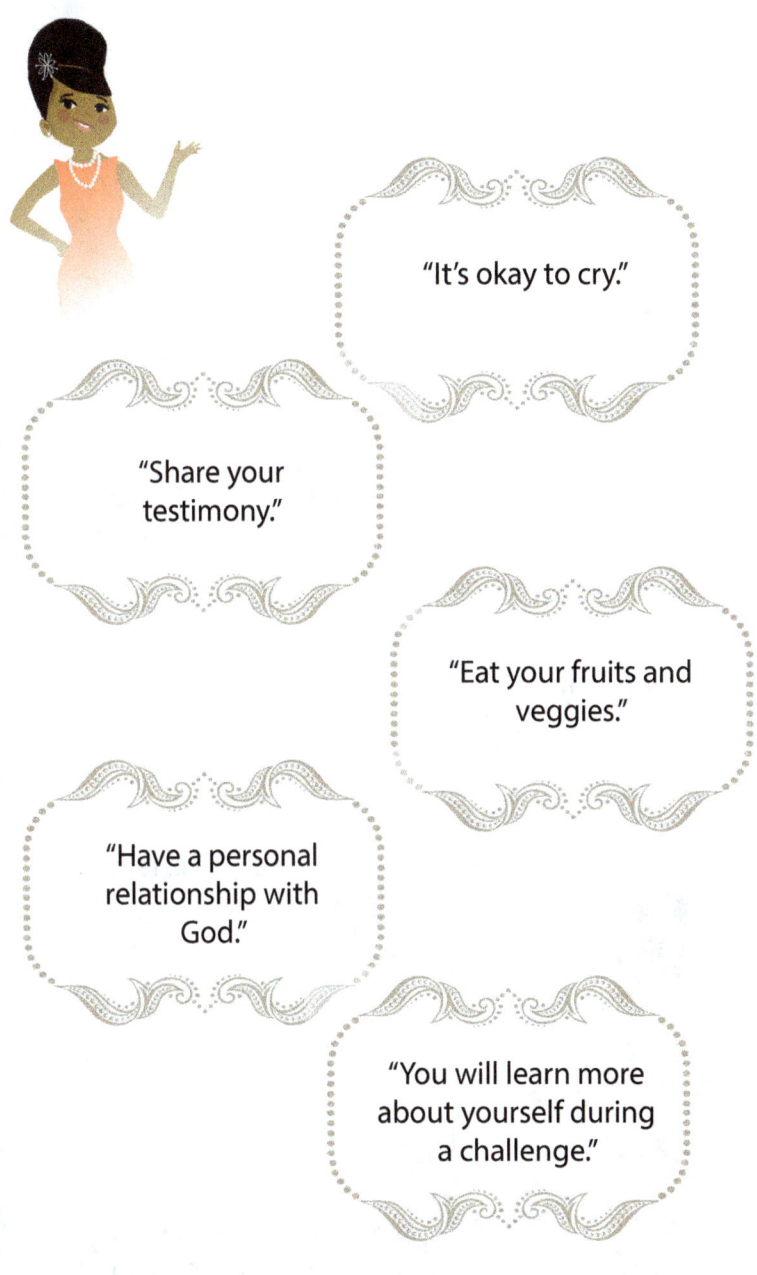

"It's okay to cry."

"Share your testimony."

"Eat your fruits and veggies."

"Have a personal relationship with God."

"You will learn more about yourself during a challenge."

"It's not about you."

"It's already done."

"Ask for wisdom*

"Enjoy the rain."

"Respect yourself enough to walk away from anything that no longer serves you, grows you, or makes you happy."

My Mama Taught Me Better Than That!

"Dance a happy dance."

"Keep your eyes on the road."

"Have faith."

"God will make a way."

"Your mind will always believe what you tell it. Feed it faith, feed it truth, feed it love"

"Go see a play."

"Expand your vocabulary."

"Listen to all types of music."

"Get regular check-ups."

"Expect great things for other people and be happy for them."

My Mama Taught Me Better Than That!

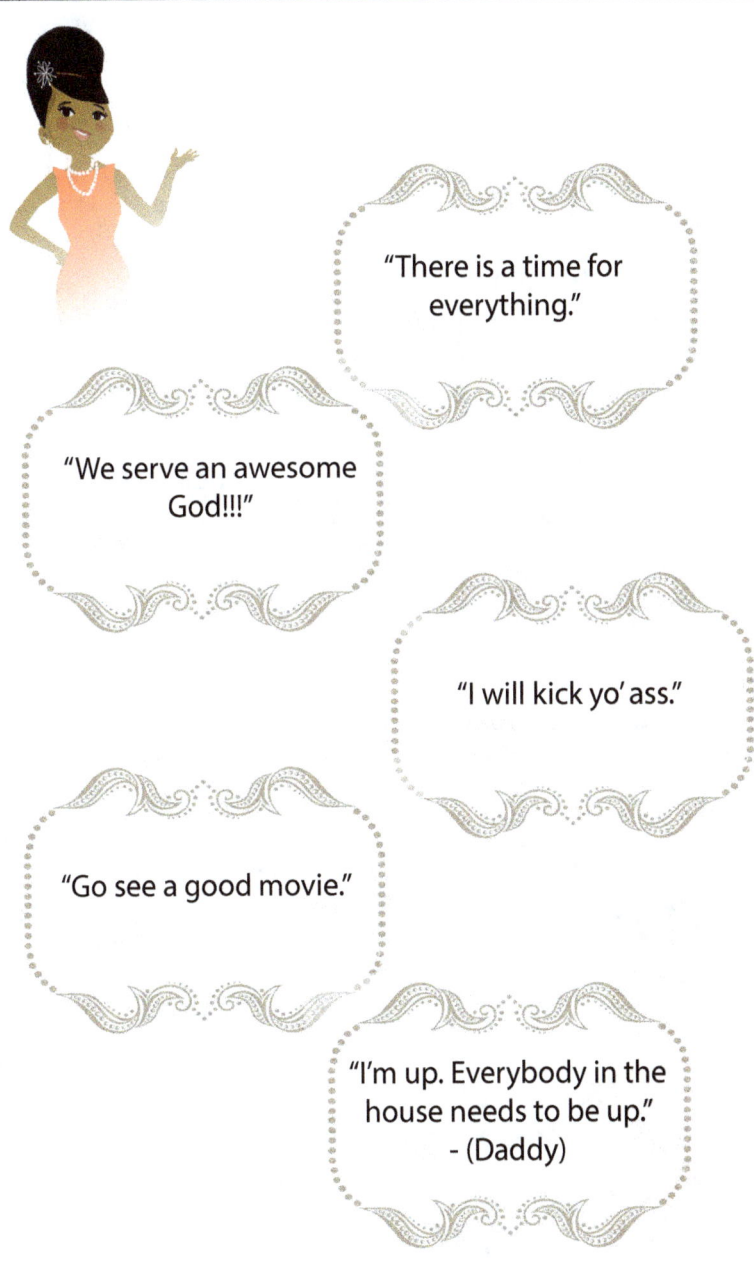

"There is a time for everything."

"We serve an awesome God!!!"

"I will kick yo' ass."

"Go see a good movie."

"I'm up. Everybody in the house needs to be up."
- (Daddy)

"Go to bed."

"Ask for directions."

"Tithe."
- (Malachi 3:10)

"Give to TBN."

"I'm so very proud of you."

My Mama Taught Me Better Than That!

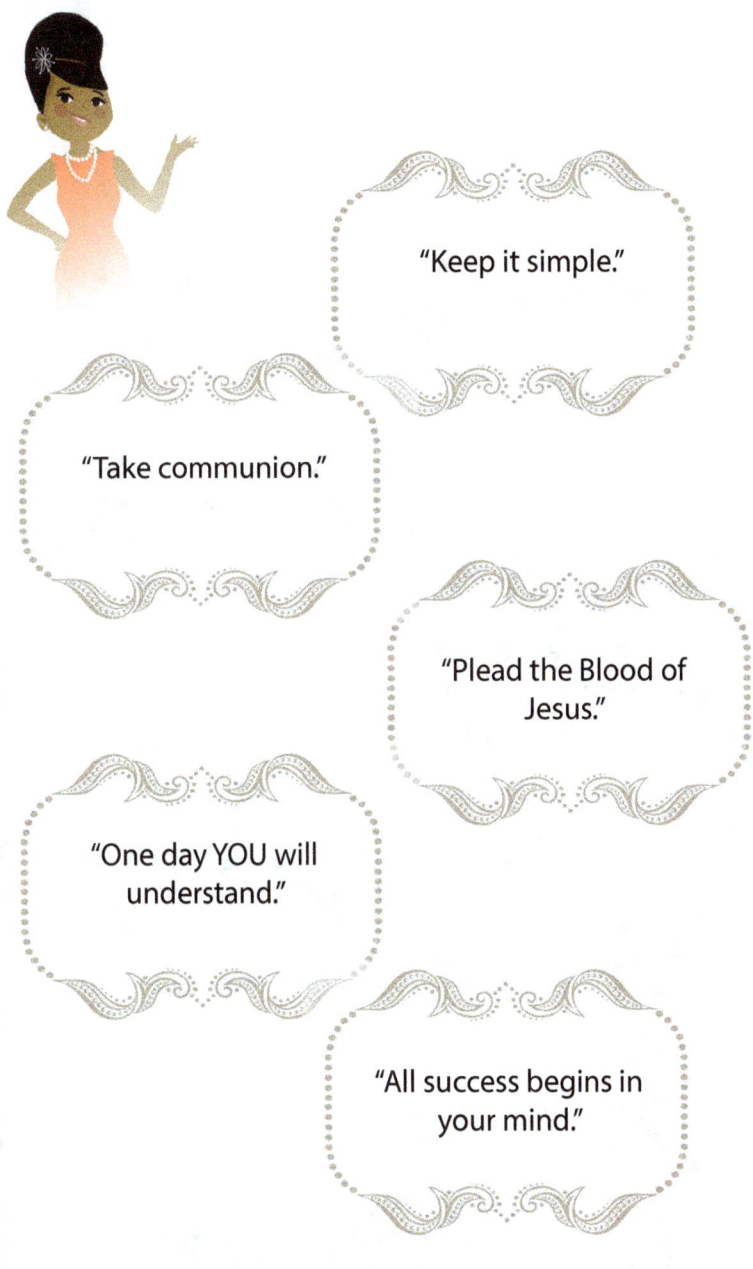

"Keep it simple."

"Take communion."

"Plead the Blood of Jesus."

"One day YOU will understand."

"All success begins in your mind."

My Mama Taught Me Better Than That!

"God is love."

"Value who you are."

"Get off the damn phone."

"Respect yourself."

"It broke my heart everytime I saw you cry."

"Get in the game and win."

"Respect women."

"Try and try again."

"Respect old people, you will be old one day."

"Live long, finish strong." - (Gloria Copland)

"Have a vision for your life."

"Prosper."

"Negative information is always free."
- (Jessie Duplantis)

"Grow daily."

"There are no overnight successes."

My Mama Taught Me Better Than That!

"Show up and keep showing up."

"Clean your toilet."

"What goes on in this house stays in this house."

"Keep your dress down and your panties up."

"Shut the hell up."

"I would do it all again."

"Pick yourself up."

"Nothing beats a fail but a try."
- (Tommy Robinson)

"Follow instructions."

"Love is a compromise."

My Mama Taught Me Better Than That!

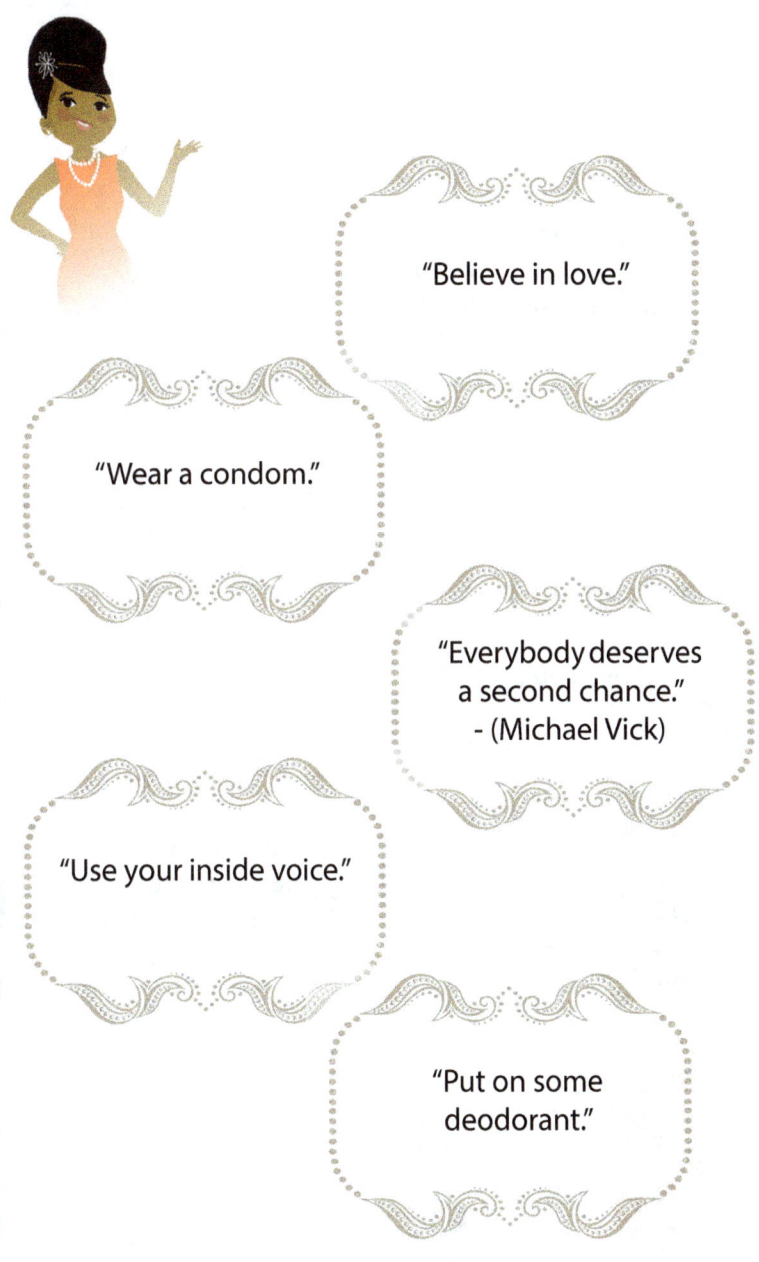

"Believe in love."

"Wear a condom."

"Everybody deserves a second chance."
- (Michael Vick)

"Use your inside voice."

"Put on some deodorant."

"Hard work never killed anybody."- (I heard someone say this on TV)

"Sit like a lady."

"Close you legs."

"Your reactions determine the outcome."

"Wear clean underwear ."

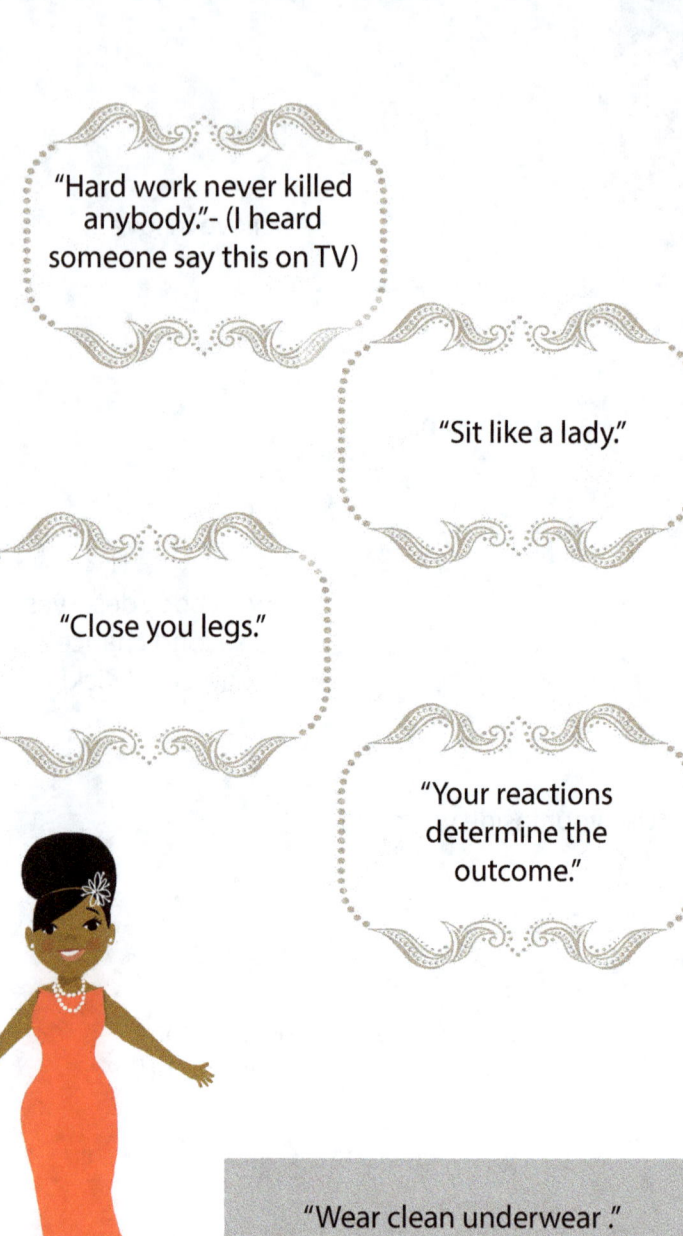

My Mama Taught Me Better Than That!

"Act like you got some sense."

"I expect the best from you."

"Sit up straight."

What God has for you is for you."

"Stop rehearsing what happened in the past."
(Bishop Eddie Long)

My Mama Taught Me Better Than That!

"Reach Higher."

"Never let them see you sweat."

"No good thing will be withheld from you."

"Help somebody else."

"Live in the fullness of God."

"Greater is He that is in you then he that is in the world."

"Learn how to network, work the room."

"Live with a purpose."

"Create an income that will keep growing."

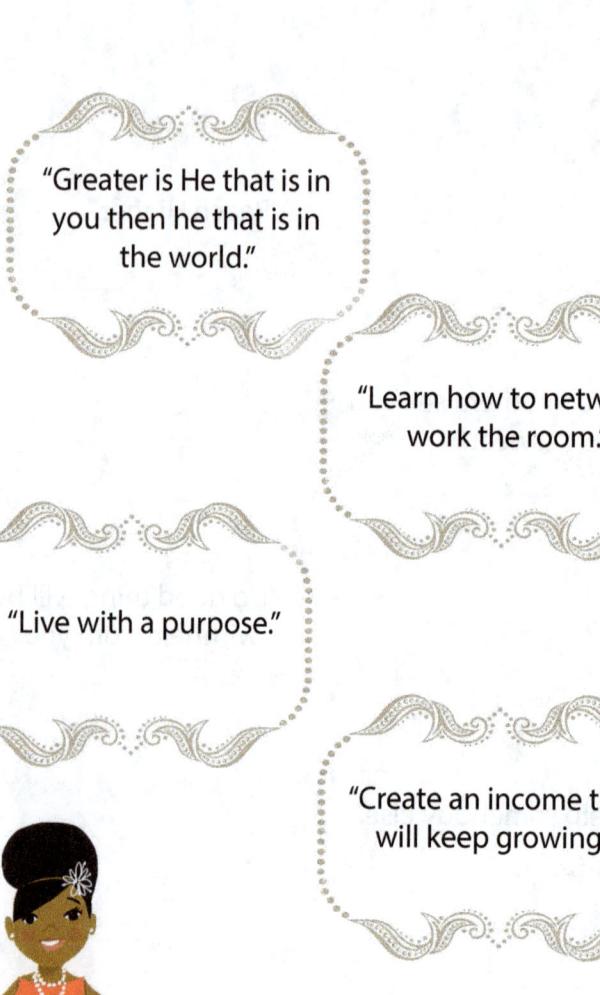

"Goodness and mercy shall follow you ALL the days of your life."

My Mama Taught Me Better Than That!

"Live today!!!"

"Find out what makes you different."

"Our God is BIGGER than any and everything!"

"Take a chance,"

"There will never be another you."

My Mama Taught Me Better Than That!

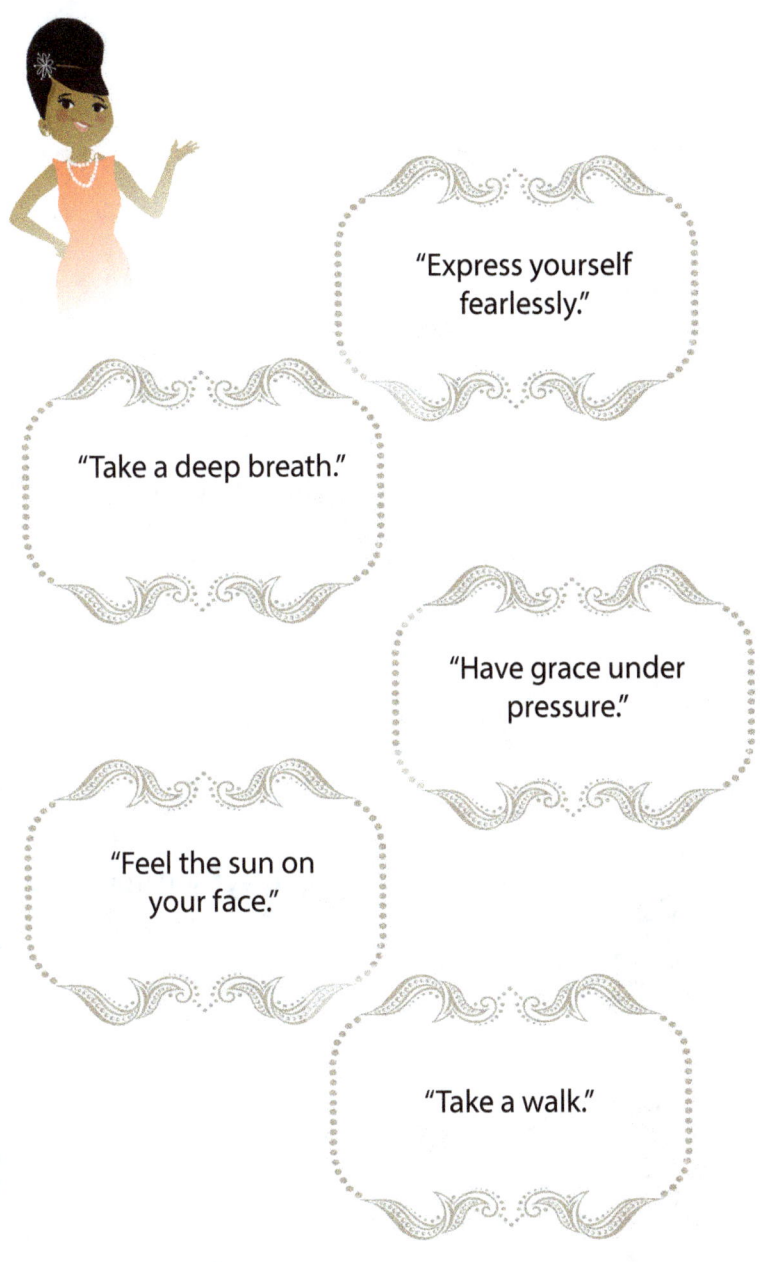

"Express yourself fearlessly."

"Take a deep breath."

"Have grace under pressure."

"Feel the sun on your face."

"Take a walk."

My Mama Taught Me Better Than That!

"Study the word of God."

"Pull yourself together."

"Stay on your grind,"

"Everything that looks good ain't good for you."

"Always think of what you can do, not what you can't."

"Sharpen the saw (Learn something new to better yourself)."

"When you are at your lowest, praise the Lord."

"Think win, win."

"Go the extra mile."

"What is that I smell?"

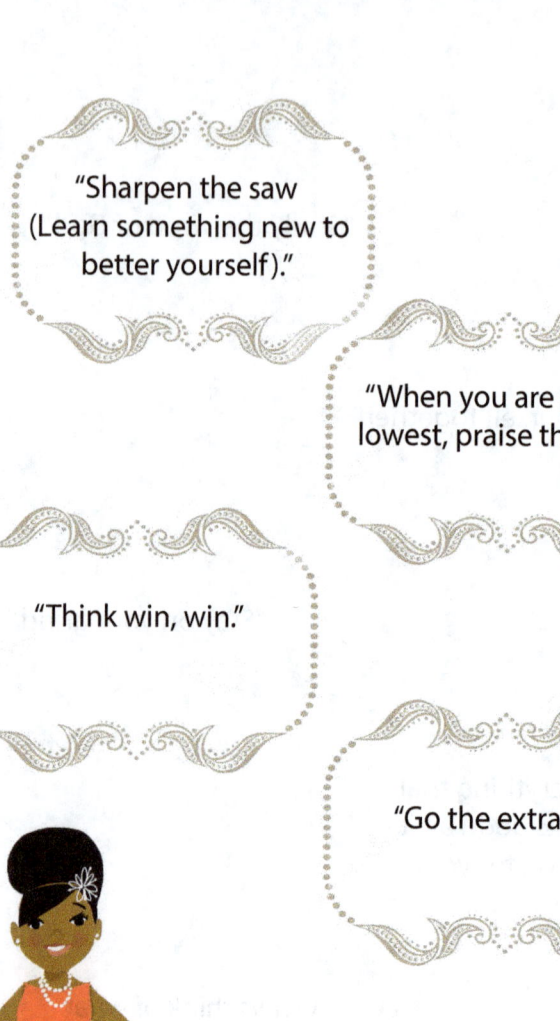

My Mama Taught Me Better Than That!

"For me and my house, we will serve the Lord."

"Keep your grades up."

"Stay humble."

"I am proud of you."

"Been there done that."

My Mama Taught Me Better Than That!

"If you don't have anything nice to say don't say anything at all."

"Look both ways before you cross the street, then look again."

"Give me a hug"

"When you get your own you can do what you want."

"Every bill up in here got my name on it. This is my house, you just live here."

"Character will take you a long way."

"Keep your hands to yourself."

"Only give money when you don't need it back (Well, it depends),"

"Money will destroy the best friendships."

"Dreams do come true."

My Mama Taught Me Better Than That!

"Set realistic long and short term goals."

"Keep fresh breath."

"Take your time young man."
- (Sylvester)

"When you fall get back up."

"Stop complaining."

My Mama Taught Me Better Than That!

"I don't have a money tree in the back yard."

"I am not the taxi driver."

"Where is their ride?"

"Why can't you find a ride home?"

"Why do you like him/her?"

My Mama Taught Me Better Than That!

"Didn't I just feed you?"

"Where is my child?!"

"Stop calling my name."

"I know damn well you didn't just slam that door!"

"The path of life is In His Presence by the Blood of the Lamb."

"Get better not bitter." - (Kimberly Dawn Griffin)

"Make new friends and keep the old."

"Speak life into everything."

"Joy comes from what you know."

"SMILE."

My Mama Taught Me Better Than That!

"Learn something everyday."

"Try to see God in everyone."

"Clean your ears."

"Love yourself."

"He is not the one."

My Mama Taught Me Better Than That!

"I'm your Mother. I LOVE YOU

"Where is your homework?"

"Go with your gut feeling."

"Good job!!!"

"I can hear everything."

My Mama Taught Me Better Than That!

"Expect great things."

"Love is the only thing that lasts forever."

"No one is perfect."

"Create great memories."

"Stop and take time to enjoy the moment."

My Mama Taught Me Better Than That!

"It's never too late to start over."

"Goodbye does not mean forever."

"Live a life you can be proud of."

"Take your time."

"It's okay to cry."

My Mama Taught Me Better Than That!

"Expect great things."

"Prayer really does change things."

"I knew you could do it."

"Give it to God."

"Whatever God tells you to do, DO IT!."

"Play to win."

"One bowl of cereal should do."

"With love all things are possible."

"Know what purpose you serve."

"When you forgive, it's not about that other person, it's about YOU growing past it."

"If you want to kill it, ignore it (Say Nothing)."
- (Serita Jakes)

"Run your own race."

"God will help you bring it to pasts."

"Learn to keep your dreams to yourself."

"Some people can't handle your dreams."

"I would not suggest that."
(Yvette)

"Think before you say it."

"Surround yourself with people who will make you better."

"Be true to what God put in your heart."

"The best relationships are the ones that make you better."

My Mama Taught Me Better Than That!

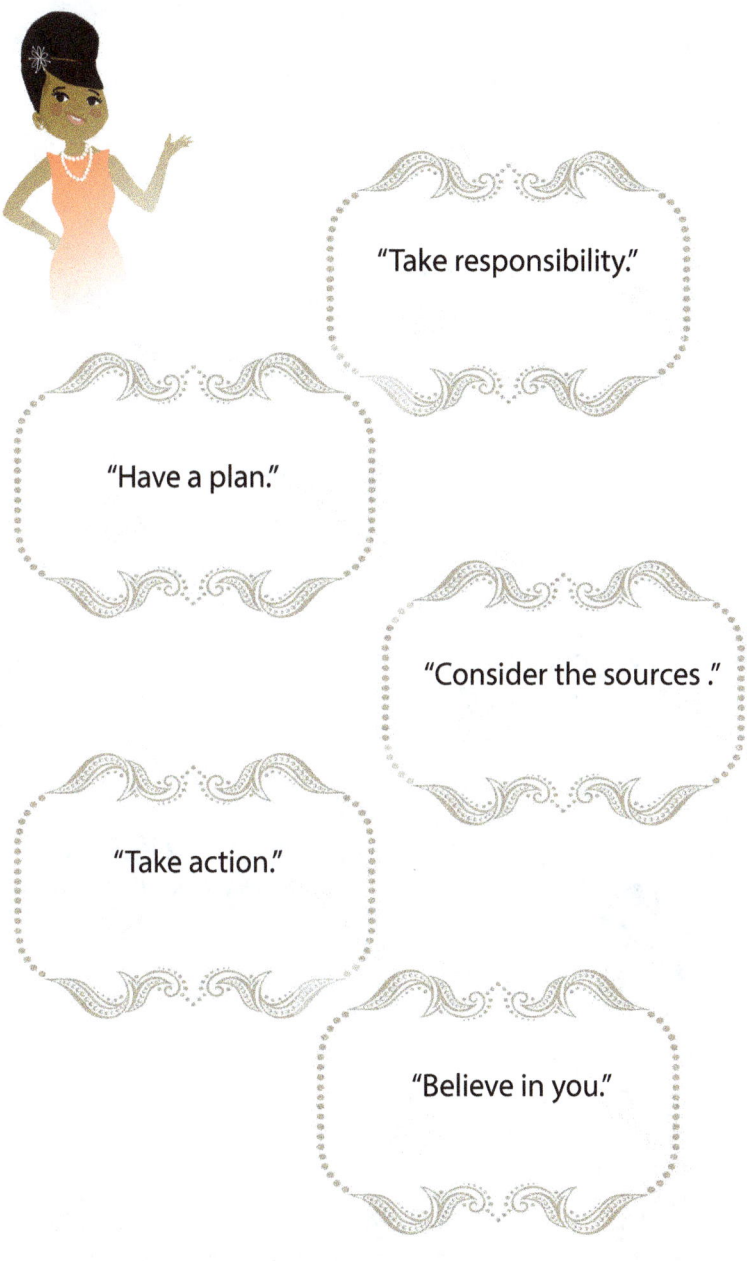

"Take responsibility."

"Have a plan."

"Consider the sources."

"Take action."

"Believe in you."

"Hold your head up."

"Let go of your fear."

"Give good hugs; they have power."

"The best project you will ever work on is you."

"Life will push you to your knees."

My Mama Taught Me Better Than That!

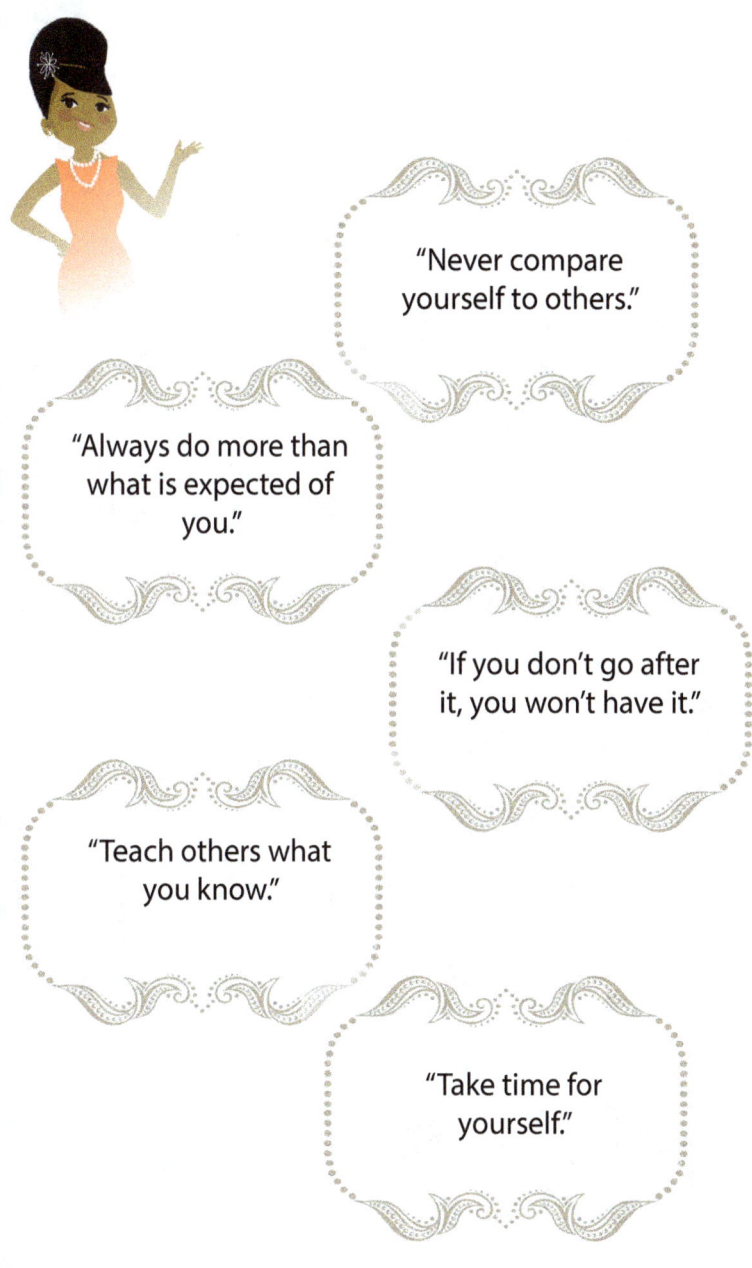

"Never compare yourself to others."

"Always do more than what is expected of you."

"If you don't go after it, you won't have it."

"Teach others what you know."

"Take time for yourself."

"YOU..."

"You will see it when you believe it."

"You are the ONE. This is the place. Now is the Time!"
- (Paula White)

"You bet not EVER!"

My Mama Taught Me Better Than That!

"You can't wear that!"

"You have no idea how much you mean to me."

"You are a Giant killer, A game changer."

"You are reasonable for YOU."

"You be the leader."

"You are Amazing."

My Mama Taught Me Better Than That!

"You win every time."

"You are NOT always right."

"You make me better."

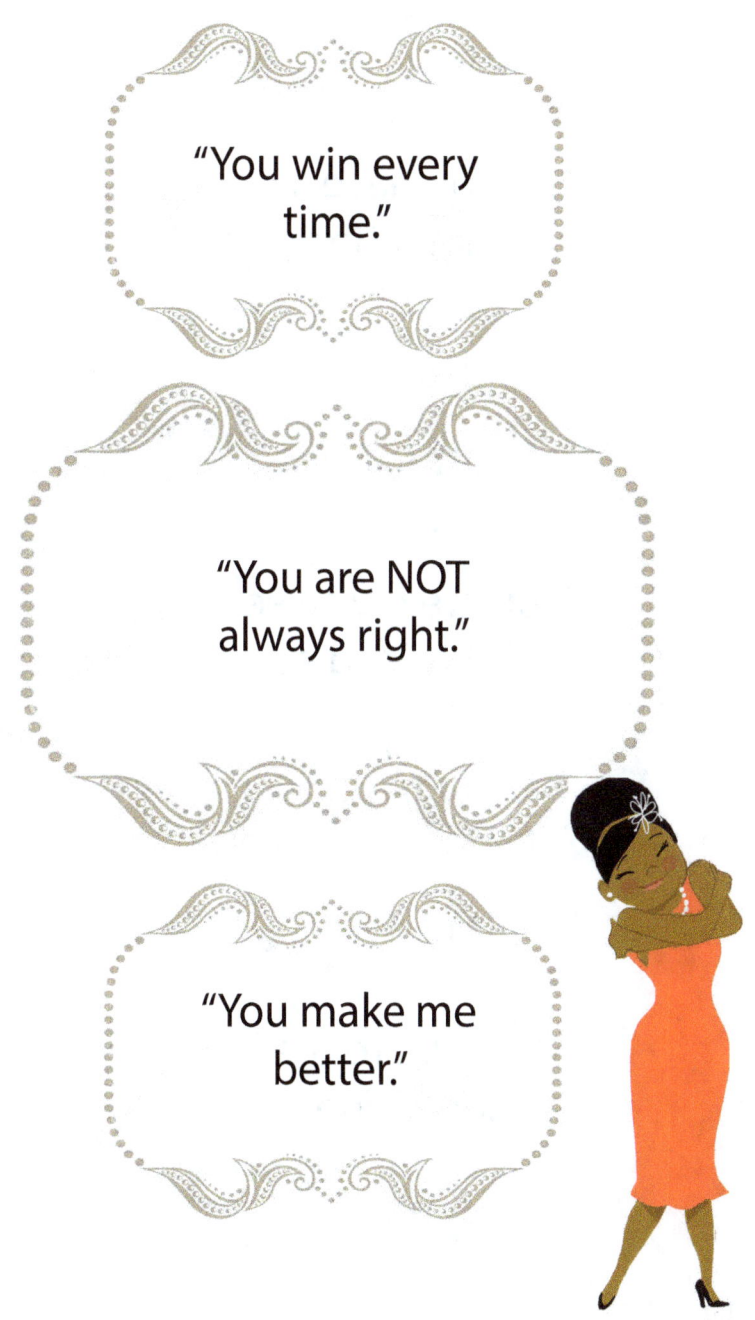

"You have a great imagination; use it!"

"You are my sweet baby."
- Madison

"You are the best son in the world."

"YOU have to believe in yourself."

"You don't have to go to every party."

"You are in control."

"You can change."

"You don't need casual relationships with people who mean you no good."

"YOU determine the outcome."

My Mama Taught Me Better Than That!

"You are creative."

"You have it all inside of you."

"You are never alone."

"You are special."

"You are the head and not the tail, above and never beneath."

"You are victorious."

My Mama Taught Me Better Than That!

"You live in my heart."

"You are FREE to be you."

"You are handsome."

"You can do it!!!"

"You have increase, wisdom, structure and favor with God and man."

"You, Be strong."

"You have ALL power."

"You will be grown soon enough. Enjoy being a child."

"You are more than a conqueror."

"You are a champion."

"You can learn something from everyone."

"You are an overcomer."

My Mama Taught Me Better Than That!

"You can always come home."

"You are acting like you have no home training."

"You are unique."

"You have what it takes to win."

"You can always come to me."

"You have Jesus."

"You are wonderful!!!

"You can talk to the Lord. He does hear you."

"You are beautiful."

"You have power in your words."

"You have uncommon favor with God and with man."

"You bring joy to my spirit."

My Mama Taught Me Better Than That!

"You will always be my child."

"You don't have to like me but you WILL respect me."

"You know damn well…"

"You make me so proud."

"You don't have to impress anyone."

"You can start over."

My Mama Taught Me Better Than That!

"You can change the world."

"You don't work, you don't eat."

"Your reactions determine the outcome."

"You are extraordinary."

"Our God is BIGGER then any and everything!"

"You are not your father."

My Mama Taught Me Better Than That!

"You are brilliant, talented and strong."

"You're almost there."-
(The Princess and the Frog)

"You are chosen."

"You are your worst enemy."

"Your thoughts are a powerful thing."

"You are smelling yourself."

"You will know when I tell you."

"You have come too far to stop now."

"You don't know everything."

My Mama Taught Me Better Than That!

"Your face will get stuck like that."

"You become what you believe."

"You have lost your mind!"

"You can't do what I do."

"When you get your own, you can do what you want."

"You are anointed."

"Your great-grandmother was awesome."

"Your father is missing the BEST part of his life by not being a part of your life."

"You WILL do great things."

www.ingramcontent.com/pod-product-compliance
Lightning Source LLC
Chambersburg PA
CBHW050639300426
44112CB00012B/1862